FOREIGN VOICES,
NATIVE TONGUES

"While reading <u>Foreign Voices, Native Tongues,</u> there's a feeling, you're back to back with the poet. The words here have you vulnerable but you love it. Melanie Perish talks to you of then and now. She talks to that belief of future you in the pursuit of self and community."

Andrew Romanelli, recipient of the John Oliver Simon Award

FOREIGN VOICES, NATIVE TONGUES

Poems

Melanie Perish

*For Nancy —
Whose voice is always
welcome. (Your wit, your
humanity. (and your words
always inform mine.
Joy & respect,
Melanie
04/2022*

Madrina Editions
Single Wing Press

Contents

For

Jon and Cheryl

The following poems have appeared
in the publications listed below:

After Reading an Article
  on Particle Physics — Brushfire (Fall, 2017)
America the Beautiful Revisited — Emerging Poets
(Z-Publishing, 2019)

Beliefs at Breakfast This Morning — di-verse-city
(AIPF Anthology, 2018)

Black Coffee, White Peaches — The Meadow (summer 2021)
Casa Tierra — Brushfire (Spring, 2016)
Collaboration: Desert and Dance — Collateral & Co. (July 2019)
Duet — di-verse-city
(AIPF Anthology, 2018)

Fat Chance in the Land of COVID-19 — Nevada Humanities
(December 2020)

Kinship — Notes of a Daughter
(Motheroot Publications, 1977)

Learning to Fish: Live Bait — Sinister Wisdom (1981)
On Death in the Land of COVID-1 — Nevada Humanities
(December 2020)

Sometimes the Ranch — Emerging Poets
(Z-Publishing, 2019)

Steel — 13TH Moon (Fall, 1983)

The Carnival at the Surgical
  and Pain Management Center — 300 Days of Sun
(summer 2021)

We Are Not Always — Sinister Wisdom (1981)
What the Godmothers Told of Origins — Persimmon Tree (2020)
What the Godmothers Told of the Pond — Avocet (Summer 2019)
What the Godmothers Told
  of Their Writing — West Trestle Review
(January 2021)

Wheeling — Brushfire (Fall, 2015)

The Body and the Body Politic

"A constitution, in the American sense of the word, is a written instrument by which the fundamental powers of the government are established, limited, and defined, and by which these powers are distributed among several departments, for their more safe and useful exercise, for the benefit of the body politic." -Samuel Miller Freeman

"The body is the instrument of our hold on the world." -Simone de Beauvoir, The Second Sex

A Disfigured World

After Adam Jagajewski

Try to praise a disfigured world.
Remember the cloud suspended
mid-canyon, gray as wet ashes.
Thimble berries on the edge
of the scorched orchards – sweeter
that any of their cousins.
Remember the way bunch grass reclaims
the old hunting trails planted by ghosts
of crows and the Quem who are no more.
You must praise the disfigured world.
You've seen border guards shake their heads,
asylum-seekers wander, then sit and rest.
You saw three silver planes climb the night sky
their wing-lights like the brightest of animated stars.
Two arrived, and one became a mass coffin.
More than once, you've heard minor chords
resolved into a major key like sleep.
Remember us – our July – each week
the old quilt spread out under a park
sycamore. Recall the unvarnished nails,
the agile fingers of a middle-aged woman
plucking mandolin strings. You put all our coins
into her coffee can on the walkway. Praise
the disfigured world with its random variables,
its infinite integers that locate planets and stars
that shine visible and invisible night and day.

On Death in the Land of COVID-19

After Cesar Vallejo

I will die in the mountains on a hot day,
on a day in May, July, or October, but one
like today with no vaccine, still air, trees
as busy with photosynthesis as I am with death.

This day will include words in lines less jagged
than a granite ridge, less smooth
than beach glass, but varied as shadow-lines
on the bright ground hard with rocks and choice.

They will say, *The poet chose not to start the clockworks*
of her heart at Three Horse Flat near Five Lakes.
Everyone knew she'd forget to keep the mistress-key
in her back pocket. Hearts attack. Ventricular contractions

don't always respond to voice commands. The witnesses
are Black women, pilots, miners. They include
brook trout, cairns – a mouse caught in hawk's talons –
or the magpies that eat death and fly.

American the Beautiful

Suppose we re-write patriotic; suppose we reconsider *America
 the Beautiful,*
the glorious and famous anthem the late 19th century left us. Suppose
we take the *for spacious skies, for amber waves of grain*
from Atlantic to Pacific and acknowledge the phallic stalks,
purple peaks and the Christian-approved mandate
of Manifest Destiny that pushed us West.

Suppose we agree the Dominants projected all their white defects
onto black and brown people, sanctioned genocide and colonization
from ocean to ocean and later from Earth to moon. Suppose we
characterize this anthem as vainglorious and infamous as the egos
that celebrate it today with their torch-lit hate,
 their ignorance of the difference
between sexual and sexual assault. Suppose we explore new pools
 of words,
glens of words, high deserts of words to fashion out-of-fashion
 suggestions.

Suppose instead of the large, we consider the patriotic of small: the
marmots as well as the elk singed to ash that sky-rises in summer fires,
or pay attention to damsel flies drowned in river-rolling floods
moved from every one-hundred years to every other year.

Suppose that variety and difference were celebrated as much as size,
force, reach? Then perhaps America would not be building
a border wall, but gates where first entry is given to those who hunger
for possibility, or the mountain-bellied mothers who know we live
 the miracle
of blood and the sea in each of us – from sea to shining sea.

Cups

She chooses depth, grip, the ability
to hold heat before color, texture, age. Heft
is important because it's more than weight; it is
the relationship both have to gravity, to light
and lightness. Her world relies on sips and lips.

Danger: Under Construction

The salesman's car is candy-apple red, parked
near the model houses. Coreopsis – wild
with dark petals – will subvert the just-laid
asphalt. Indian paintbrush, poppies vie

for purchase with sharp-tipped foxtails.
The gas-powered saw – round
and hand-held – whines fine dust, cuts
through driveway brick. Already the thin bones

of tumbleweed, the blond cheatgrass
would flare with one spark. This box canyon
holds sage and greasewood
that hold these hills together.

The rattler unwinds herself, smooths
down the brick-pile – silent as poppies.

What the Godmothers Told of the Thirteens

The thirteens live with hot, latte-hearts and snow-cone blood,
sometimes catch their tears in small basins, keep them,
and douse the flames of meanness that comet to parents
or friends. These become the long, wide sighs of restraint,
firebreaks in Confusion Foothills. They can be tungsten-bold,
steel-stubborn or pliable as Tussar silk draped
across bruised peaches. Their bodies hurl them
like boomerangs or halt them still as Autumn air.
They have to do what they have to do while they want, and
some want to do what they want to do right now –
even though time is a blood moon, fox teeth, fire light.
So often the thirteens ...

Beliefs at Breakfast This Morning

I believe everything important begins
in the body. I believe reading makes you
beautiful and no lives matter until Black lives
do. I could never be a psychiatrist
or an electrical engineer. Giving time
is hard and gratitude, an action word. I believe
friendship is the organizing principle
of my life just as honesty is my core value
and forgiveness, mandatory.

My rules for travel demand companions seek silence
and solitude and allow me to do the same – that conversation
include laughter and opinions
both as welcome as mutual respect. I believe
all birds are female and all antlered species
are male. I have faith in the conscious choice
of poetry, the healing properties
of walking uphill in trees and other prayer.
I believe love powers us and fear drives us too often
which is why I count my breaths for a while every day –
and sometimes grace and a pale blue appear.

Duet

She was slow to welcome
the walk with him –
season of edge

and bare branches,
estate of hard ground, iced ponds,
trout with slow tail fins.

Behind her desk too long
she'd forgotten expanse
was love – like sky crystals,

rendered in short
wave-lengths long blue
over peaks and wings.

A forest of pine and fir,
the wind-pleated snow he showed her,
showed him. Again.

Invisible, silence sounded like
trees breathing and she could hear
their two-four time.

He'd forgotten, that after dark,
the quiet between them
could be caught and colored

by whatever moon
pinned the horizon
into place.

After the Firewatch Reports, September 11, 2020

More smoke in the air
and I grieve for California.

Everything else in my life
shrinks to dust motes when

towns and trees burn
to ash. Nineteen years ago,

smoke and ash in New York City,
in a field outside DC – but Bagdad,

Beirut, Paris, Nairobi, Hong Kong – all
with their own moments of great

devastation, horror. Some days I am
as tattered as this world.

I don't think of raindrops,
kittens, copper kettles –

I think of you, reader,
somewhere. May you be

at ease. May mercy find us camped
wherever we are in the firelight.

Haiku with Titles on the Day of Delayed Departures

Fate

Three women sitting
On a stalled flight talk to each
Other. Great cats roam.

History

A woman who will
Not lie is a danger. They
Say, *Burn her, burn her.*

Daily Tasks

Reconstituting
The world, we go to work, we
Put the child to bed.

Charlottesville

We're told to love each
Other. They march with torches
And guns. Shouting.

Qualities and Quality

Her work and children,
Her dog and job, her poems
Are strangely the same.

Summary

Three women sitting
On a stalled plane listen to
Each other. Flight rules.

Juries

After Rita Dove

1
A helmet's strength.

A shout up close.

A plea for reason.

A window smashed.

A call for prayer.

    A fire.

    A right.

2
Assault
involves
two.
History
involves time,
attention, multitudes.
Justice involves
inter-
being.

3
within the palm
  and the touch
within the foot
  and the kick
within screen lies
  and good sense
within jail
  and cell
within fear
  and freedom

often
within.

4
Proof depends on who
offers it, who
receives it, how
doubt can bloom
in who –
  one
  both.

5
Reorder the daylight;
turn down the babel.
Dusk dims into night.

In every hour, the waiting hours
  until the winds slow
  until the floods drain
  and we can hear
  the words
  that are
  true.

In El Paso: August 4, 2019

The angel of death
is young, male, white, and Christian
and he has a gun.

Still alive, he kills
himself with every victim.
Who is his Christ?

The angel of death
has a manifesto: it
is racial cleansing.

Still alive, he's shown
shock, confusion, no regret.
Who will be the next?

The angel of death
hunted Latinx, hunted
people with brown skin.

Still alive, they say
he's cooperating. What
can that even mean?

We

After Claudia Rankine

have been the sellers, the sold
  the girl's blue bruises under her shirt

have been the man in summer
  the gun of his failure

have been the gun in his rib cage,
  shot and wounded, been wounded

have been the needle in the flesh,
  hands that pushed poison and rush

have been a river's rush and run
  a river run with poison, spun its current

have been a woman defined
  by a body, a body for birth

have born a body, made fine
  and redefined by women

have been inspired, spiraled
  down, buried, been buried

have been a story
  and unstoried

have been a dialect forgotten
  mispronounced or mistaken

have been a love that reserves shine
  and wears textured shadows

have taken, have given,
  been forgiven

have been the will to change
  opening like the iris of an eye.

Wheeling

Driving, driven. Bartleby the Scrivener knew and like him,
we *would prefer not to* and yet we do and know and do
again. Drive, driven. Like Chicago pols: Drive early; drive often;
even the dead drive and we do drive dead: dead-heads,
dead-headed for gardeners and herb connoisseurs alike.
It's better, we'd say, *than driving dead drunk,* but it wasn't.
Driving, driven. Under the influence
we drove in droves – not just under the influence of substances,
but under the influence of not-substances, of the insubstantial,
of concepts, the concept of crossing or the cross.
We put the *trans* back into transubstantiation of the soul,
of the sole artist or the soul artist. Is there
any other kind? Yes: the sold artist. Drive, driven.
Behind the wheel of a sedan, a compact, a sub-compact,
   a trans-compact contract
that may delineate the conditions
under which we drive or thrive or we survive
despite the obvious driving we do in hazardous conditions –
not only rain, sleet, hail and dark of night – but with others
as any driven creature.

Anxiety Attack as Lesson

For Audre Lorde

The chapter on snuff films,
the *other* –
unspeakable cruelty.

I'd just read, *Truth and the body*
share structure, when my heart

beat faster than aspen branches
in any breeze.

Cadence is my life
on the page and off. The in-and-out
of the lung's bellows did what self-talk
could not.

Were blood vessels narrowed?
My scalp – tighter
than those chin-strapped swim caps –

stung me. I am stroke-worthy.

But my blank-verse brain
with throb and no meter, listens
to ancient women
spleen-lodged and awake.
I've learned

the ancients don't sing incantations,
rather intone a sensing –

pine pollen wind-lifted
in columns across canyons.

Black Coffee, White Peaches

She sips coffee first: dark roast, ebony, a flavor-shift from tongue
to throat like chord progressions in Ellington's *A Train*. It takes her
back to the city. Next, the white peaches: firm, juicy, unpeeled.
The fuzz returns her to women dancing, last call – to a terrace
on a co-op overlooking the Hudson. Upper West Side. Dawn.

After Reading an Article on Particle Physics

Smaller than the piece of lint
she watched him brush off his shoulder,
or the piece of grit
he took out of her eye
with the point of his linen handkerchief,
or the single grains of superfine sugar spilled
next to the Gold Medal Flour
in her grandmother's Hoosier cupboard.

Smaller than a hadron
and its electromagnetic charge,
or the quarks racing their
infinitesimal colors inside it.
Quarks can't be seen
by the most powerful microscope;
they can only be seen in motion.
This is the moment that love starts
and desire.

What the Department Store Window Told the Old Woman

After Clint Smith

Don't use me for a mirror – I can't help
what they display behind me – neither can you.
There's always some group that wants
to display an old woman:

see the difference this eye cream
makes on these lines below the eyes?
Or *help–help I've fallen*
and I can't get up.

Most think we're both transparent,
me – wiped clean to better show
the merchandise. I'm
part of an economic marker. You
are a well-researched demographic.
They know we break, but they forget
we lacerate, too. Some days even
the politicians forget us, but I
persevere and you vote.

Here you are, walking
in a mid-sized Western town
watching yourself in me. You cannot see
the lines beneath your eyes. You
have not fallen, yet. You still shine.
You're sharp. They think
they can see through you
as they see through me.
They haven't factored in light,
contended with reflection.

The Day after the Midterm Elections 2018

Extravagant sky. So much
blue. The pond

Lacy with leaves, two mallard males
tuck beaks under wings.

A hedge of cattails
stands straight, blonde,

The brown brush-tops
seed next year's lances.

Everything is turning
into something else,

Doing the lush bidding of the gods
who took steps to protect America today.

Alienation

after Charles Simic

Alienation cannot fathom the solitude of the archipelago.
but understands the island's isolation.
Does it swim or tread water?
Does it recognize Karl Marx and the relationship
between the worker and the product?

Has it always been global and local with homes
in Jerusalem and Tulsa, Prague and Nagasaki?
Does the dandelion in the sidewalk crack
remind it of itself?

Will it dwell in a dark city apartment,
or a farm that grows corn
and nightly dreams of leaving?

Can it be present in the schoolyard bully
and the kid that gets stuffed in a locker at lunch?

Does it ponder the ignorance of privilege
for the light skinned and the vigilance around it
for sepia-skinned people?
Does it love its bed and refuse to get up or
does it sit munching chips and sipping soda all night?

Is it armed with a torch and American flag
or a sharp tongue and a rainbow banner?
Can it enter any place of worship
and hear its calm?

Does it see us as the elephant of strident witness
or the spider with its silk of mute silence?

Will it swallow us whole.

Kinship

You talk of anger.
You with your black hair
darker than storm clouds crowding
over the steppes,
dark as the hair of Russian women
who planted
who baked brown loaves to feed warrior husbands,
who blessed their sons
with the sign of the cross before battle.

You write and
do battle,
feed yourself,
bless daughters with these words:

      they are sharp blades
      they are chants more ancient
      than the cross.

      When you talk of anger

      plough down castles,
      turn over the prince,
      the princess dead in her sleep,

      the Russian mothers before you
      become your bones, your eyes,
      your black hair.
      I see you planting
      breaking ground.

Learning to Fish: Live Bait

You hand me a night crawler
from the bait box   pull your own
long and active from the pellets
of moist soil. I watch you
stick the hook-point into the worm
inch it 'round the bottom barb. You ignore
the flailing head   the squirming tail   the gut ooze
that muddies your fingers.

Kids catch these at night   you tell me.
After a rain   with a bright moon   they take
flashlights   flash the ditchbank and grab.
You have to be fast with your hands
and pail. The worms are quick too
wriggle right back
into the wet dirt when the light hits them.

Street lights hit me.
I ducked into shadow of poles   squat signals in the railroad yard.

I was	The yard boss never caught me
small and a girl	his daughter went
so I was fast	to a different school
a quick mouth	his flashlight hung from his belt
I lied to save pokey Sasha	the nightstick too he wore it
in the yard	carried the storm lamp
I swiped coal	he grabbed old hobos asleep kids
from open box cars	shinnying up hiding running

He called us all night crawlers.
You bait them   my father railed. You give them
excuse to call us   hunkies   thieves   to say
your people lazy   no work. Someday they break
your head   break laws in new country   break
my heart. My mother used the coal I stole

to cook soup   burned it in the heater stove
near the room where we all slept.

You finish baiting your hook. I begin
with mine   stop to remember   some species
struggle alone. I expect blood trickle
the muscled twist of live bait. I'd fight too
to keep from dying.

What the Godmothers Believe for Lovers

Lovers need the miracle of bodies
stunning as falcons that mate in flight-freefall,
selective as grey wolves and their strong thighs,
uncommonly common
like whales belly to belly,

Lovers need the patience of a mugo pine unlovely
and shaped like a hassock. It grows squat
and steady. Patience perseveres like the water
that cuts a new creek bed and rushes rock smooth
without care for the cadence of its current.

Lovers need witnesses
consistent as long-time friends or black oaks
bright as the Pleiades in November –
witnesses confidential as canyon boulders who know
their role is to watch and listen.

Lovers need grateful words, mutual quiet,
daily forgiveness or short memories. They need
the dialects of silence, the reverb
of humor, and alphabets of whimsy. All lovers
need the language of tongues
and nothing else.

Age on a Curious Day

"The great thing about getting older is that you don't lose all the other ages you've been." -Madeleine L' Engle

"I live in that solitude which is painful in youth, but delicious in the years of maturity." -Albert Einstein

Song of the Road

I walk beyond the dead end
of the road. Blonde grass mashed
on grey dirt not as dark
as the ebony bark of fir, the soaked
black branches made more visible
after rain. Smell of sage is
as intense as color now.

If fir and sage fused into an animated hand,
appeared as a holograph that drew a new and instant trail –
it would not surprise me. The magic of the what *if* lives.

How many roads do we conjure? How many
come to us by accident or through strangers?

If the conjured trail remained, the one drawn
by the holograph hand, I'd walk it with you
or alone. The trail does not
know my limitations: female, skeptic,
a pin in the left hip, as I do not know
its destination, its response to a half-moon,
its winged residents or footed travelers. The trail
is only a trail despite its spectral origins.

It is the variations
I want in any road: its incline, way-stations, its language,
its boundaries, its potential
and mine.
I want to do what I honorably can do
as I walk its history in my present.
The lesson of choice is never ending –
and when the road and the lesson join,
that is the song.

Discovery after Decades

(1)

Five mornings before Christmas,
we smooth bottom sheet, top sheet,
pull blanket and bedspread tight –
pillows cased and shammed on your side, my side.
All this before we get into bed again
under the polished-cotton quilt,
under well-worn chenille –
the heat-blended current along the length of our bodies.

We are careful. Old fractures pause;
new pinched nerves wait along the spine's corridor
and tell us we are old.
As if we can't see this daily,
as if this means anything
in the wrinkled eyes of wanting.

(2)

Two people together for decades
know the need for forgiveness:
to forget the knife-edged voice
fresh from the whetstone,
to ignore the roar
of a flash-over temper

People need compassionate words
or no words when one
wants the bedroom window
open in November and the other says
a calm nothing and finds another quilt.

We two-step through these days
of your ventricular contractions,
of my fracture poorly mended,
find that pulse or pull, heart or hip
are among ways that explicate
this ratio of the body's pain
to love's failures. Let's sigh,
lie down, skin on skin.

(3)

Walking uphill
is as close to prayer
as we get. I often pull you
into habitats not named
obligation. Tree trunks with
branches bent toward the ground
wear mastodon faces
with either-side-juts for tusks.

I stop while morning
rises over hills that cannot
balance the sun between them.
The forest is where we traded
some open questions: Where
is the place of death
or life? Self or service?

As we start on the trail,
you pull me into you.
Light dapples the ground like clear
leaded glass waiting
for a saint to be puzzled into it,
or a doe to bless it, or that last look
on this earth to be a sun-studded trail
for one of us or the other.

At Seventy-One Still

Contemporary of rebels, writers,
those whose tolerance honors
sentient being, the vote, and those
who vote with their feet.
You seek enclaves of honesty,
consideration. In them
there are men and women with avian kin
rich in wings, song, the sky's democracy
when America fails us.
Like ytterbium – that element
used to aid portable x-ray –
you reveal bone: living frame
that holds, protects,
moves us to the truth
in what we choose to live
before we turn to ash.

Fat Chance in the Land of COVID-19

Where are those moments of high desert calm?
This land is a world on tilt. A world on tilt rings,
lights up, keeps score, and wants calm.

My calm is a privileged calm. It's a calm set
in a small city, is aided by a body temperature read
less than 98.6 degrees Fahrenheit coupled
with a three-day break from shriveled blossoms
and hard freezes. Calm is coaxed into sight
with ruby sunsets, Nevada blue days, and finches
at the feeder – or the last Zoom meeting
with co-workers/classmates/friends/family
where you see a screen of faces smile
from postage-stamp pictures
talk to that little mic in the left-hand corner
sometimes with the red backslash through its spleen.

In the fourth week of COVID-19
my old white woman, middle-class calm
is conditional. It depends on whether I've watched
local news, national news, news that's 24/7.
It depends on how much fear
anyone should allot a small elevator that houses
two movers not wearing masks and their proximity
to your closest friend and her grandmother's tri-corner table.
The move to assisted living complete, you both
will count the days she remains symptom-free.
Calm depends on reports from friends of friends
who are self-quarantined, run low-grade fevers,
have a lover who is an EMT and not getting enough sleep,
or a father that waits for a ventilator in New York.

This land is a world on tilt. A world on tilt rings,
lights up, keeps score, depends on the strength and force
that shakes the pin-ball machine. It depends
on the players: federal and state, economic and medical.
A world on tilt wants calm.
Fat chance.

Hags

My old women are hags
and rise with rutted-cliff faces and once-muscled
bodies whose skin hangs like a spotted beige sheet
on a clothes line.

I admire the way they avoid mirrors
and like the way they stare at their own faces when
their reflection's found in windows
by accident, the way they smooth

the arch of an eyebrow, touch a mouth corner
and smile, glad to make their own acquaintance again.
Eagle-eyed, hags search
wind-scoured mountains or each other.

Incredible-credible is their timing,
their instinct for when to look and look away
like old doe in forests – stock-still until
the hunters are gone, then leap
fallen fir trunks from a stand-still,
bound without sound into deep cover.

Hags teach us awe –
they take hag and make it a new
species of old women. Haghood is a residence of irreverence.
They know time is time and a hawk's hooked beak.

Five Ways of Looking at an Old Woman

1
The desert blooms.
The old women
wash their faces.

2
Old women turn toward
each other now and before. These
are natural formations.

3
I do not know which to prefer,
an old woman who is fed up
or an old woman who speaks up.
The moment of clarity
or clarity given voice.

4
As the three old women left, the nurse whispered
Obeah-woman, bruja, oracle, Shiva, hag,
shaman, harpy, Kwan Yin, godmother –
and these are only some of their names.

5
It was afternoon sky at sunset. The clouds
promised glitter rain in the distance.
The old woman wept. And why?

Amends

There is so much I don't know. At twenty-five
spending the day often ended in finding a way into
a bedroom with double paned windows, flowered
or navy-blue sheets; legs longer than mine,
my sleep deeper, my falling asleep after sex
more immediate. *Please forgive me,* I said

and never meant it because I never stayed awake after
or stayed. I couldn't get to know anyone because
Dewar's White Label was waiting for me at home
offering me that break from the perfect labor-force report
the celebration of another promotion and so young.

Does it matter that with help –
I have lived differently? Today
I'm not sure – and god is silent.

Traveler Now and Later and Now

I die and my poems – with stunning words
or failed lines – will fade like summer curtains in sunlight.
High desert dust is my witness and the wind
that excites it. That wind bullied the cottonwoods yesterday,
but walks among them now to make amends.
It does not regret the past, nor wishes to shut the door on it.
Neither do I.

Learning discovers itself in different synonyms
for *find*. I find a new dialect of silence: stillness
after a brother's last breath echoes the stillness
of grief felt five years after. Acceptance
is a breeze through aspen and appears like age-spots.

I will die in a friend's living room on a curious day.
I will cup a mug of tea in both hands and glance
at a framed calendar from his grandfather's long-ago business:
Tiscornia & Ivers Funeral Home
Mariposa–Merced.

Outside the sky stands tall in dark and dove gray,
where god sends birds and insects for comic relief.
A scrub jay dances on a juniper branch.
A swallow-tail lands on the lip of a blue iris:
mariposa–merced. Butterfly-mercy here
and here.

West on the Lake Road, Mt. Rose, Nevada

I drive West on this road for the lake's silk surface. Its light surprises.
Its quiet can quiet me. The two-lanes curve beneath weight, wheels,
and spinning treads. The pavement – sometimes smoother, sometimes
raveled – climbs toward the summit: a glimpse, then a glance, and a
view of its stretch and ranges.

You offered me this
road, hum of pavement, boulders
at road's edge, silent.

Wind chants through fir. It same-note sings through sun and shade
splayed on the road. Strong breeze dusts road shoulders, the metal
guard rail and its squat wood posts. Wind here has a history. These
granite mountains, eroded by slow-moving ice, finally felt rain sluiced
between ledges.

We were friends for years.
Both moved in geologic
time toward each other.

I slow just past the summit – park, then sit and breathe. On the
far shore, the snow-bright mountains slide into the wide base of
their own reflection. Satin more than silk today, this lake's surface is
stitched with beads that flare and spangle.

Jays in light-slants ask
in sandpaper calls when you'll
return? Soon. Yes, soon.

The Carnival at the Pain Management and Surgical Center

After the injection of steroid medication
into the 7th cervical vertebrae, my eyes
couldn't touch the ground.

> My smile felt like the one I had
> after making out with Jimi Collins
> at the July carnival in Tinley Park –
> my car, not his. Jimi
> played third base, could hit,
> had a good arm, and good hands.

There'd been a release in my shoulder blades quick
like a bra unhooked from behind with one hand.
An aid told me to just rest for a while. Did I want water?

> Eyes closed, I wanted to follow accordion music
> piped from a Ferris wheel to black pegs
> from the ring toss, to the tilt-a-whirl lights
> Jimi and I passed on the way to the car. I remember
> the way he looked – in an Auguste Renoir way – lavender light
> in his blonde hair, dabs of cranberry, a slash of gray
> in his madras shirt, the blurred button-down collar.
> I felt his breath on my ear, and then

when the nurse put her hand on my hand,
I smiled the idiot-girl smile
before she asked me how I felt
now.

What the Godmothers Told of the Dead

The dead live in mountains,
in smoke swirl, sun's flicker,
or the trill of shadows on a two-lane road.
The dead miss their bodies
even though they like the diaphanous drift
similar to the smoke that calms bees
as the keeper examines her hives. The dead calm the living
this way, especially those who want to follow them
into the grave, the urn, the crypt, the loose ashes airborne
over the Thames, the Truckee.

The dead whisper and linger on blush-colored buttes
like the taste of salt echoes on the tongue.
The dead morph into shadows blurred or sharp that ride
like clouds through groves and short meadows
slotted between Castle Peak and Red Mountain.
The dead rarely rest on iron-veined boulders
or mica schist rocks, even the rose quartz
hikers stop to touch. The dead miss their bodies,
but they like the court and spark
of their change to light, those shafts that slide their gold
down to ground, sift it to flaxen fire that's fused
to mid-fall leaves. Yellow, that yellow
evoked by light on the visible spectrum.

The dead say this hue is simply that gold
all other sights of gold control.
They would know because for eons
the dead wandered. The mountains
welcomed them, kept them, taught them.
And the dead have given the mountains
lessons in the physics of mystery.
Not carefree, they live the gentlest form of grief:
the dead miss their bodies.

Found Poem: Postscript from Cheryl

What is with
this cycle of tens?

1959: I go
to Hawaii. My mother
dies.

1969: My father dies. I meet
Lucian. I go
on my first trip
to Europe.

1979: My grandmother
dies. I quit
my job. I go
to a women's writing workshop.
I meet Melanie and Sallie Ann.

1989: Lucian and Melanie and Sallie Ann
reunite. Some of us
travel. Some of us
have jobs. All of us work.
No one
dies.

Midsummer Ritual

Close the screen door
behind you.
Give thanks
and close your eyes.
Repeat the name
of one of your dead.
Hear the light and
taste it
as if it were
a slice of fruit.

Let ideas fall to the ground
like bird-dribbled seeds
from the portholes of the feeder.
Breathe in faith; breath out fear – unless
it's the right moment to hear
what each has to say to the other.
Do not envy the eyelashes of the llama
or the winter coat of the arctic fox.
Open your eyes. Count the shades
of green and invite your voice
to say nothing until you have
a single word that you hold
like a prism in your hand.
Does it have – what
does it have?

Iris Present and Past in the Land of COVID-19

I prune dead iris each morning
from every one of three vases.
The double blooms in blue, the twin yellow buds –
one open and about to flower next to
one spent. The petals of these are
like balls of tissue paper wet
and crushed into themselves.

I email a long-ago lover a photo of iris.
*I feel such humility, she writes back. The doctors here
are very good and so good to me. Amy is, too.*

In the afternoons her brother calls her,
asks for body temperature, the relative difficulty
of her breathing. My mind's eye sees us younger
hiking near Monitor Pass. She's in her navy
camp-shirt and khaki shorts, step after step,
switchback after switchback. She stops to survey
the high field, searches for iris wild and violet.
I stop too. We are both thirsty. We say we love each other.

Foreign Voices, Native Tongues

"All objects, all phases of culture are alive. They have voices. They speak of their history and interrelatedness. And they are all talking at once!" -Camille Paglia

"Why does the lizard stick his tongue out? The lizard sticks its tongue out because that's the way it's listening and looking and tasting its environment. It's its means of appreciating what's in front of it." -William Shatner

We Are Not Always

We are not always the wise woman
the staunch healer, the constant midwife,
the one who culls the herbs
into the magic poultice.

We are not always mother and daughter,
the strong hands, the nipple's sweetness,
the arms that rock and rock
and give when need demands it.

We are not always earth and water
nor two sheaves of wheat,
nor shells wet with repetitious waves
the salt rim fresh on the thin smooth lip.

Sometimes we are the spinsters
who turn the wheel, but do not spin,
the mother's nag, the daughter's wanton anger.
Sometimes you are the river,

the river that threatens my field;
I am the wave that hurls its crest
like rocks
against your clapboard beach house.

Like atoms
we move,
owning weight, mass, momentum.
We are not always anything but ourselves.

What the Autumn Peaches Suggested to the Old Woman

They call us autumn flame and we
see you know the turning of autumn,

that your skin, like ours, might be
more thin suede than the velvet plush some

think we should have. Time's become
another feature found outside and under skin.

Flesh is flesh after all, and yours thrums
with blood-pulse while ours commands

smooth fibers with what's sweet –
land of the round and nectared.

The sun feeds us both,
fuels the juice

that's in us or has been –
juice that leaves chins dripping.

Chrysalis

accept you are a seeker
no longer afraid
to admit you pray
to sit in silence listening
to embrace men and women
that drew you to nakedness
always
with shadow-coves
and the discipline of hope

you live hard-shelled, near the creek bed
pulled to flight
to cardinal flowers
the passion of whirling water
the rush, the falls
and the quiet ponds
calling
insistent smooth temptation,
swallowtails
wet-winged and suspended.

A Reader Says

Poets and titles draw me today. They pull me
up into their landscape. A phrase, an unexpected
line-break hike with me, power up the switchbacks
that plump my calves and make the pump of my heart
work hard. Their words burrow into my days
like moths in leaf litter.

Once last year, in this body among *foreign bodies,*
I dreamed *the black unicorn* came to me, told me
to learn the dark, to love the dark
even when *the dark takes aim* because *darkness
sticks to everything* – and it takes great release
and grateful effort to commit to acts
and ways of being in the world you never
imagined. She told me it is then
I am able to enter into *the hot climate
of promises and grace,* where I will know
*a wild patience has taken me this far.**

*Attributions; Foreign Bodies, Cheryl Lundstrom; The Black Unicorn,
Audre Lorde, The Dark Takes Aim, Julie Suk; Darkness Sticks to Ev-
erything, Tom Hennen; The Hot Climate of Promises and Grace, Ste-
ven Nightingale; A Wild Patience Has Taken Me This Far, Adrienne
Rich.

The Story as Told by the Trail

I know the cadence of feet and the privilege
of open spaces. I live on stolen land.
In spring, I am sun-seeking. I mud the soles
of boots, make the suck-sound new
and know some find it ugly.
        In meadows I bask and wait
        for wild aster or iris, paintbrush
        or California poppy. Stone-studded, dusty
        in summer and fall, I ramble, I wander –
        is it any wonder I am
        who I serve?
I came into being long ago through the instinct
of mule deer and the hunter's
skill. They traveled the untraveled and made a way.
Like an old woman, I retreat in winter,
cherish the snow-loaded silence and feel
weight above me like a lover, like the memory
of lovers.
        In the forest, I am in the company
        of trees. Their roots reach and sculpt me
        in ways that surprise us both – like time.
        Meadow or grove, I persist. In any season
        the night sky is close – as close as death might be.

Ode to a Short String of Lights

> "Everything has/ a mother, a father, and a story."
> Judy Grahn, "The Inheritance"

Everything can be of use; and you are more
than decorative. Cathode and anode, each battery

has its snug place in the circuit. Electricity
via chemical reaction courses lined and aligned through

a copper wire. LED beads of bright that in the right night-dark
might ping shadow dots on a bookshelf or sideboard.

Mother of Invention is not necessity in your case
of creation. More serious than whimsy, you are

a tiny tangle and annotate the inky dusk around you. It's
no surprise you articulate well. Someone's

father, kin to Father Tidy, shuttered you in a cupboard –
unaware you thrive in all seasons. Glad

and sadness pivot on the misinterpretation
of purpose. I've had opportunities,

a few chances to revise the lives of underserved things: a dangly,
feather earing paired with a star; a strip of silk as bracelet. To

story is my intent today. To pause and listen to
your dialect of silence. Out of nothing, something.

Minnie Mouse

I hated the polka dots and the too-short
skirt. Then, the bow between my ears. Really?
 Yellow pumps clearly too large and perpetual gloves
instead of hands made less sense than me
coupled with that narcissist Mickey.
I was never cut out for Disneyland or Hollywood.
Places with so many slick surfaces were never
real for me. I may be two dimensional, but I'm not
two dimensional. I'm a country mouse at heart
and the ranch is where I returned, of course. No one
in the truck garden, in the house cellar, under the back
porch ever believed the lame cartoon plots. I come from
survivors. The idea of rescue (over and over)
from gorilla or gaucho, from death by fire or drowning
were ways to praise the dominant species,
to reinforce what passed for creativity
in the large and lumbering. Keen-eyed nesters,
adept at foraging, field mice were too
complex to draw, took too much time.
I want to scurry, not dance, chitter, not sing
in some Western-themed eatery with a liquor license.
More later. It's time to find that hole in the siding,
the one that opens into the kitchen.

Steel

The locks of mill buildings, the peaked roofs,
the double row of dim windows
stand straight as a foreman;
the huge knuckles of pipe
fist their steam into the night.

The women know the yawn of the orange furnace,
the dead eyes of men in the lunch line.
The molten ore splashes,
seared with coke and flame,
unlike the flicker of votive candles
where they pray for the lost pension,
the supper stew, the safe birth.

The billets of steel thunder
and tough with tungsten
forge the beams, the scaffolds,
the huge coils of pipeline.
The women hear these
each in her own dreams.

From the slotted lights in the mountain houses
they watch the stars slip
beneath the river, the hazed moon,
the mill that looms across
the Allegheny bank –
the alloys of grief and will and silence.

Near Here, I Remembered

Now the water's low
    the cattails seeding
launched into the air
    past fence rails
that try to boundary
    piles of dredged stone
and my mother
    remembers the water
its silver surface

*weeds exceed me** and
    even as blackbirds cluster
on the lone live oak
    into the tangle of raspberry canes
trees and tall grass, stone
    left from the gold rush
remembers these ponds
    and the paper reeds,
but does not remember me

*Theodore Roethke

What He Saw Wheelbarrow Watching

1

The wheelbarrow is a boat
that won't float, a front yard
flowerbox with day-glow geraniums
in dark potting soil. It's a neighbor
to a faded red wagon beside the garage.

2

Scarred, the wheelbarrow is
a great-uncle who disked a meadow
with a tractor, but remembers
a pair of horses pulled the spring-harrow
before he could seed the field
below Windy Hill.

3

The wheelbarrow is a cousin
to the iron-pronged rake that leans
against the shed wall like
a straight-backed parson
with a wide, toothy smile.

4

To Jack-and-the-Beanstalk giants,
the wheelbarrow was always
a decorator piece – useful
as a place for rings next to a sink,
a caddy for paperclips
on a desktop two miles long.

5
Once sky blue, its secret is
it's never wanted
to be a red wheelbarrow
and cares nothing for chickens.

6
Today, the bucket
has nothing
in it.
The wheelbarrow
is full of empty.

Disconsolate Lines

For Tim Jones
After Jane Cooper

Because a stand of mountain ash is sliced by sharp light.
Because the hummingbird feeder belongs to the greedy bees.
Because all six neighborhood dogs bark
 to out-loud each other and I woke myself mumbling
Oz, the great and powerful and didn't know why;
Because aspen and oak turn gold and crimson
while California poppies quiver in fields.
Because no hard frost means stems and branches
        rattle leaves filled with change and capillary action.
I am in confusion, lines drowse in my mouth, I sense
        not more than one stanza that's awake,
        and not rendered from a dream.

It is true my friend died in the fall five years ago
and I mourn. No house fell on him.
By the Bay in a heart-stopping city, his heart
        stopped. His brain went slack and his courage
        became a tornado of recollections in many minds.
This is nothing he hoped for.
I knew him to be a wizard – not behind a curtain, not
        in a peddler's wagon in Kansas, but a seer of possibilities
        with a compass he would lend you.
Grief has no rubied exit, no emerald place to pause, only words today
        near a stand of mountain ash, great and powerful.

Note Passed to Mary Magdalene
After Lucille Cliften

You were always my favorite: Mary of Magdala,
Mary Magdalene, sometimes simply Magdalene.
I called you Magda and prayed to you, too.
Long overdue, this is a thank you for your body,
for being present in it; validated by your seven demons
cast out or not. For befriending Jesus, investing in him
and a cause that shifted toward love.

Thank you for being the apostle to the apostles
whether any of that dozen noted it or not.
Thank you for keeping watch over Mary, blessed
mother, for walking and standing with her
on the day of the crucifixion, for your deep
listening after it was finished.

I do not know if Jesus rose
from the dead. I do not know if you, too,
saw an angel on the third day. But I have heard of women
who came to a tomb's entrance, saw the floor-length wings,
a luminous face and form. They nodded in his direction,
asked that he step aside so they could enter –
listened to one another.

Self-Portrait as Cell Phone

My roles – like apps – are chosen or assigned:
citizen, friend, Calm, Merlin, writer,
godmother – calculator, calendar, clock. I
am keeper of contacts, pictures at an exhibition
or not. Text and outlook have always drawn me,
told me, been part of journey and evolution. I am
lambent in a bright kitchen, a dim dining room,
even getting ready for bed. I am not always
easy to find favoring as I do basic black
with pops of color. Tantalum, like a sharp tongue,
can be toxic, but resists corrosion, elemental
to survival. Without rest or proper current-connection,
I die slowly from lack of charge or fatigue born
of repetitive motion. I am information, although I
contain opinions, and a range of emotions in phrase,
in photos, in videos. The present is a galaxy
of connections, biometrics, security, complete
with system updates. Change is electric.
What else to do, but follow suit? I fit in time's pocket.

What the Godmothers Told of the Breeze

June breeze yawns in the face of trees,
tired from the walk over the mountains,
and a brat to show distain for cones, leaves,

and bud color. The breeze is only a slow wind
with naked admiration for its strength to carry pine pollen
up and over knolls on the Mt. Rose Highway.

Welcome or not, June breeze sleeps
here and there, naps in limbs and branches
that carve strong angles, lines that beguile air.

Awake, it traces the lower lip of a cloud's
nimbus like slender fingers. It warms
water surface like openhands

before rippling the Truckee into a river of wrinkled foil.
June breeze is a flirt – sometimes gladly invited in
through screen doors or windows, sometimes

closed out when someone wants to block
its ease, which is often when this breeze,
tumbles through tall grass loose-limbed

with its transparent and scanty freedom.

What the September Dream Told the Old Woman

You need to collect more of me. Haven't you
always found unexpected questions in the dark?
The rush for lush impossibilities? Still,
sleep made word can toggle between story
and image like skywriting.

In dream time, singularities shine like glossy still shots:
a barking spaniel, the hummingbird's green zip caught.
Most nights your eyes seek surprise
like early apples. In August, you wanted
jewels, saw them on a velvet-lined tray.
Each gem was luminous. Tonight, similar stones
are animated. They speak. The ruby
longs for an intimate flight on a swallow's
peach breast or gray scissortail. Why not?
You have had your share of avian night rides.

You are drawn to me as I am
indispensable to you, and the wander
we both enjoy. In me you leap
treetops like Douglas squirrels
or swoop air where dawn falls.
Several of these breathe fire.

Some nights, paths veer, intersect,
vanish like sandcastles. Old lovers at crossroads
compel touch: a hand on a shoulder, a light
kiss on the left cheek. I am dream
and random matter – the time traveler –
you are the moment empty,
                sign-less,
                        impermanent.

This Morning Life Said

Present company included
welcome to your room —

bright as an opal wall
behind a woodwind quartet
or winter starlight above a wild forest —

Everyone wakes with differences,
everyone wakes to miracles
in the moments and inches
of one more day with this sun, there
beyond cirrus clouds
sailing.

Death is coming over later
for tea and the view.

What the Shy Streetlamp Told the Old Woman

1
The streetlamp
is a popular place
for any god
to leash her griffin

2
The streetlamp dreams
of a shooting star, a swan's neck,
luminaria suspended
from its slender pole.

3
The streetlamp
watches over the sidewalk
and listens for the quiet
between footsteps.

4
The streetlamp is an inverted J,
a calla lily stem with a white bell blossom,
a booklight for a giant
of any gender

5
You should know
a streetlamp
is not
to be
taken for granted

Failed Poems

Last week I wrote only failed poems and
in verse both free and blank, in words that formed
no form at all. There were no lines that I
could see worth stealing. Inverse image, snapped
and snappish yielded verse not versed in much
at all. How's that for specificity?

The haiku was
seventeen syllables without
nature or seasons.
The haiku was just
seventeen leaves without stem
drifting on no pond.

The sonnet by Will Shakespeare locked its rhyme;
In each and every line the meter shone;
The closing tried so hard time after time
To sum the thoughts, but broke instead like bone –
Off base, off kilter with no centered core.
I wrote, but faltered, fell and wrote no more.

Today I try again, watch
my sister's cat, her gold eyes studded
with onyx ovals smooth
with meaning.
She paws the patio glass
in two-four time for sixteen measures
and stops,
like this line;
waits – like any poem –
for the way out.

What the Godmothers Said of Writing

We no longer ski downhill, edge to edge,
hair streaming like first draft lines. We trek
in spring's cold, spot the odd snow-plant, pink
as cotton candy spun in the sky's kettle of gray clouds.

Snowshoes strapped tight as a sonnet's
rhyme, we move carefully through
cedars and loblolly pine, avoid drifts like wasted
words. It should be snowing, but it's

not. We should be writing and we will,
but differently. To write, like any winter trek cuts
new trails, sometimes follows paths put down
earlier in the day or season. Some of us rediscovered

lyric lines, cadenced stanzas like the moonless night we
snowshoed the farm-field, saw stars fly, white as barn owls.

Words for Warriors

after Robert Pinsky

When I had no house, I made
honesty a cabin. When food
ran short, I ate sun from humid fields.

When my tongue could not taste.
my hands found savory on the riverbank.
When my hands went numb, I knelt in prayer.

To listen is my strategy.

When my father spit out fire
I inhaled short poems. When my mother sailed
to Saturn, I swam against the current.

When my brother died, I made
trees my friends. When trees could not
follow, I took breeze as a companion.

Mutual respect is my tactic.

When I had no chapel, I made
stained glass from gratitudes. I have
no minister; I made breathing my chant.

When I had no money, kindness
was my currency. When I lost
direction, I followed paw prints

to the indelibles and a lean-to on the savannah.

What the Godmothers Told of Origins

Distant lands close to home. Foreign voices,
native tongues – these are cell tissue
to us. Paradox is in our marrow
just as ghosts live in the scaffolding of our bones like

native tongues. These are cell tissue:
foxfire on the downed white pine. Our ancients live
just as breath lives in the bellows of our lungs like
wind is-and-inhabits sky.

Foxfire on downed white pine, our ancients live
wings tucked in after celestial navigation, real as
wind is – and inhabit sky.
Herons and fish fly, touch down,

wings tucked in after sensory navigation, real as –
to us – paradox is. In our marrow
herons and fish fly, touch down –
distant lands close to home, foreign voices, native tongues.

Indigo Place and Yellow-eyed Wild

"…resign yourself to the influence of the earth."
-Henry David Thoreau

"Leave the roads; take the trails"- Pythagoras

Casa Tierra

Returning to our casita, I see for the first time
the small row of rectangular windows slants up –
each window the size of a women's shoe box.

All four dusty panes angle toward pinion branches
and no clouds. The outside sills slant down, the wood
placed to lace whatever rain would run into the gutter.

The drain-spout nailed to the wall is no wider than two knuckles
of my index finger, no longer than an eighteenth-century woman
resting on her bed – perhaps in retreat, unsettled.

This place is hush and chant, things
complex as a loom-woven rug,
bright or faded, textured as new adobe

or smooth as the back of a Pueblo woman,
a woman who carries water, her body elegant as any vessel
that might catch a cloudburst
or cradle the wish for rain.

Indigo Place and Yellow-eyed Wild

Diffuse dust drifts unseen into us, from us.
The sky mutes itself to indigo and stars where
night birds dodge branches, skim through the taffeta dark,
mark their wildness, ask us our place in it.

The sky mutes itself to indigo and stars where
yellow-eyed owls flaunt wings, beak, vision,
mark their wildness, ask us our place in it.
We are far from wild

and yellow-eyed owls who flaunt wings, beak, vision.
Stay alert, the birds command us – *to the smallest twitch.*
We are far from wild, but we
share stardust and begin to listen, to

stay alert. The birds command us with the smallest twitch
from wings latticed and strong to see glints and
share stardust. We begin to listen, to
feel wing-wind near our shoulders, always

wings latticed and strong, We see glints and
night birds dodge branches, skim through the taffeta dark.
We feel wing-wind near our shoulders, always
diffuse dust drifts unseen into us, from us.

January: Lynx Morning

The road to the highway's piled   the field's
palmed smooth as plain sheets in places
or drifts like pillow slips and snow
snow sifts steady   blows
off the barn light's cowl   the glow

I lie in bed
don't see it but know it's true
Snow   not silent snow secret snow   No
snow sounds   It pads the ground

I hear its quiet
round as any paw   yes the fur
the fur but more
the tender underfoot
in rabbit   cat   even raccoon

all near and quick and sudden
as the snow itself   Still as any
wild thing who knows it's watched
or listened for

in the wind   My lover breathes me
back to sleep
where I hunt something
in my dreams   where I
fit the footed white   fall drifting

Sometimes the Ranch

The tall grass, willow brush, wild roses cut and dry
drifted on the creekbank. The next day, the work crew
swept them up in hard arms and together in twos, bagged them.
The water ran creek-quick, over stones bigger than chickens,
smaller than the barn cat's head. Stones set polished
in the whirring-wet tumbler so they'd shine
gemstone-bold. Days were only smooth at daybreak.
Days ran overtime, through visions that could not
be tunneled. Earth, air, fire, and water appeared, disappeared,
morphed into elements driven by velocities and currents,
angles and inclines that shaped the farm garden, orchard, herd.

Some days gave the ranch blue-black columbine,
renegade daisies or wild lilies bird-seeded
and grown tall on the pond's edge. Some days gave
blue-black clouds, renegade rainstorms,
wildfires that brought hell's heat in flame and ash.

But she – the oldest of three – likes to remember
the day, an uncle rode in
late and slow, a bawling brown calf
slung across his saddle,
the barbed-wire cuts not too bad.

What the Godmothers Told of the Pond

Call them
     water-striders, pond-skaters,
wild clock hands moving.

         Back legs steer
         middles push time's
         thin membrane, a stream's slow ceiling.

Short legs catch
     fish eggs, insects, something
to feed tomorrow and a slim body.

         These creatures and we
           live light refracted, shadows
         to track speed and weight.

Weight and time, shadows
     sharp or soft-seeming
leave us
     then leave us light.

Invitation to a Stranger in September

We could meet in the high desert,
mountains known for iron-veined outcrops,
granite not yet grains of mica and feldspar.
Incense cedar and cottonwood,
red fir and white pine started here –
in fissures rooted in change and digestible dirt.
This forest does not move easily,
but invites movement within it. We could walk

the light and shade of marked trails, discuss the grief
of every aspen reluctant to release its green. You might mention
the optimism of downed trees repurposed by wood-boring beetles.
I might suggest we stop near a creek's glissando, watch it slip
toward foothills. We could pause in the past's shadows,
listen to the imagined echo of Hokan spoken. And continue.

Watching

Birds and blank journals
open their wings,
invite flight
and fledglings,
nests woven of slender
lines of roots and root words.
There is a history
with quills. I have a history
with rhyme, with cadence,
with syncopation, with the off-beat,
the beating of wings –
and those notes held in the back
of a dove's throat or mine:
the fine print between us
unsung, unwritten.

The Wild Horses of Nevada

In the painting, the horses cross the high desert
at a gallop – at least 17 – rust colored
and chestnut, grey-white – strong withers,
slender legs with slim shadows,
echoes of movement.

Here, no clouds
march across the sky. The air
above the horizon's long mesa is a soft
afterthought.

The blue-grey shades
the wide wedge of the herd
that arrows hoof-speed on the canyon floor.
Here the world of this wild
invites me into ten shades of tawny
in a sweep of light that redefines
expanse and color.

Outcrops and hills, the dark mesa
in the distance
boundary this canyon
with a still patience the horses here
do not know.

Collaboration: Desert and Dance

Vigilance is a desert word
        with its dust,

Angles of stone;
        white domes rise

Lithe and smooth
        as legs and torso,

Legato arms of dancers
        that waist-bend like shale arches. In

Every gust, the stone swirls mauve,
        mollusk gray, the iridescent

Yellow in an albino trout. Color and shape
        flash like gesture, their movement –

Open
        as the Mohave drifting,

Falling like red silk
        across this Valley of

Fire. The desert is
        the changer and the changed,

In a dance of elements, of minerals
        that offer shades and tints

Real as the coyote, cactus bloom,
        red-tailed hawk. Here

Eternity unspools its collateral light
        weaves sun with shade, threads the white fire of stars.

Sky Inside and Out

Cottonwood seeds would drift down,
lint the June fishing line,
would pull it toward hook-point
and a quicksilver surface.

Inside the cabin,
air was swift through screens,
sifted seeds that tufted
near doorframe corners.

Outside and inside,
morning was backdrop for trout
and silence, for talk
and tea steeping, early plums.

Used to foothills and few neighbors,
my grandmother believed
she could hear the sky speak,
learned its inflections outside and inside.
Both knew the dialect of kettle steam,
she told me, more than once.
Hers was the best garden, everyone said.

Night Mirror

Mesas landscape my dreams,
prickly pear and sage.
Wild life moves invisible –
burrows, slithers, flies by radio waves
its body fur and leather.

A horizon in cordovan and dusty rose
meets a rice paper sky, its multitudes
of pixels dissolve to immaculate blue.

I coast on wings
like Pegasus – that strong.

What the Godmothers Saw of Patterns

High tide and low tide, the way rocks
grow cleft or smooth declares
the imperative of repetition. This is the bay
a water body with elements of us in it.

Grow cleft or smooth declares
the sky to every cloud. Shades of light
on the visible spectrum revere hawks.
They are hunters with an eye for the specific from

the sky. Shades of light prism colors
we cannot distinguish in sharp detail,
but attentive we hear birdsongs before summer rain
plucked from Russian sage.

Like slant rhyme, what we see is similar:
blooms seed, leaves ladder themselves like
the imperative of repetition. High tide,
low tide. The bay rocks.

Tahoe Meadows: The Story as Told by the Creek

New green
      roots of white
            yarrow,
 coral paintbrush
         web
      the current-carved banks
         held
in place. Like
        early love,
I look for
      furl
          new blooms.
It is in my nature
      to share myself. I
            racket staccato
            bubble and burst
            to shout
        spring.
Slender stream,
      I travel, ravel
        unravel –
creek source
      with force
        gravity.
Humans live
      and lean.
        Committed to clarity,
              not
      crystal,
   but translucent. I change.
          I am changed.

Long light calms me, slows the race of
      my May-June pace. In summer, my legato
is better phrased than a cello solo. I'm tasked to smooth
      and soothe the stones where tiny eggs sway,
        then spin into
        homely larvae.

Some rise as damsel flies –
all iridescent
wings
in twin-sets
on their
turquoise backs.
Like an old woman, I am shallow and deep where neither
brook trout nor striders care.
Depth is part instinct,
part choice.

Meadow grass turns gold,
lives the ground's chill more easily
than the long-toed
lizard.
Hard beaks and soft muzzles
taste frost, dip and slurp.
I am
time's talk, ceaseless
with an eidetic eye and echoic ear.
I remember
the air's voice when Hokan
was the only human language uttered.
Today's
red fox and black bear speak
the same dialects
different
from stellar jay
chickadee.
Winter is the only time I am close
to silence,
and even then,
I hum in slow
tones under snow
only the wind can move
or mold.

Attributions

Adam Zagajewski, "Try to Praise a Mutilated World"

Caesar Vallejo, "Black Stone on White Stone"

Rita Dove, "Twelve Chairs"

Claudia Rankine, "We"

Clint Smith, "What the Cicada Said to the Black Boy"

Charles Simic, "The Infinite"

Jane Cooper, "Long, Disconsolate Lines"

Lucille Cliften, "note passed to superman"

Robert Pinsky, "Samurai Song"

Maynard Dixon, "Wild Horses of Nevada", painting

Afterword

This book owes a great deal to a number of people. I hope I've remembered them all. This book has its form because of Sunny Borges. He listened to me, offered suggestions, helped me with things large and small from helping me get an ISBN number to the actual design of the book. Theresa Gabrielli once again was a superb copy editor and remains a trusted colleague and friend. For most of the past year, my work has been enhanced by Courtney Cliften, a fine poet and colleague. Her careful reading, attention to nuance, and rigorous honesty elevated a number of the poems included here.

Poetry readings with Tom Meschery at Sundance Books & Music introduced me to a poet who is as generous as he is meticulous in his diction. The speakers in Gailmarie Pahmeier's poetry have voices that I'm drawn to. Her work makes the particular universal. She is an outstanding teacher. The generosity she extends her students is remarkable. Recently, a writing retreat and workshop lead by Kim Stafford enhanced my work. His poetry incites questions and he's an abundantly careful and effective teacher.

It is impossible to be a poet in Reno without acknowledging Sundance Books & Music which always opens its space to forums for writing and writers. The Nevada Humanities Counsel has been a lifeline for thoughtful people throughout Nevada and gave us outlets like Heart to Heart – a weekly offering of experiences of the pandemic by Nevadans throughout 2020 and 2021.

Several years ago, Katherine Case of Meridian Press, invited a phalanx of people to write a poem a day for April, poetry month. A handful of us responded. After year two, five of us continued to exchange poems weekly and over time several others have joined us. Someone dubbed us the Saturday Poets. Many poems in this collection are better for the insight of people in my writing exchange: Annie Stenzel, Nancy McClelland, Katherine Case, Judith Rodby, Sunny Borges, Vivian Olds, and Patricia Caspers. Katherine Case was good enough to read the very first iteration of this manuscript three years ago and read it yet again this year. Annie, Nancy, and Sunny have consistently offered me specific and instructive critiques for many of my poems. The Mary Nork-Joe Crowley writing workshop has also played a major role in improving a portion of these poems and others that have not made it into this collection. Joe Crowley's passing was a major loss to his extensive writing community. Mary Nork and Gemma Hartley are important influences in this book through comments and their own work. In the Advanced Poetry Workshops with Gailmarie Pahmeier, students shared their helpful critiques with me. There are too many to mention. Often decades younger than I, these classmates have given me points of view, language, and perspectives that I'd never have acquired staying within my own age group. Shannon Palladino was a classmate who is fine poet, and scientist, and researcher. I'm grateful for her thoughts on my work.

One of the unexpected gifts of the COVID-19 pandemic was getting connected with a community of poets and writers in Southern Nevada. The reading series facilitated by Heather Lang-Cassera was a wonderful forum. Heather, herself, is committed to her work, poetry, and fostering community among writers. Poetry Promise, anchored by Bruce Isaacson of Zeitgeist Press included me in the weekly readings and discussion and was attended by able and interesting poets from Nevada, the Bay Area, and New York. Encouragement and suggestions posted in the chat of those monthly and weekly Zoom readings were welcome and thoughtful.

Decades ago, I was fortunate enough to enter the women's writing community in New York and San Francisco through a number of women's writing workshops started and sustained by Beverly Tanenhaus (Hartwick College), Marcy Allencraig (Santa Cruz, CA), and Kathryn Mahon Aal (Ithaca College). I am/was privileged to share work with Adrienne Rich, Audre Lorde, Joan Larkin, Valerie Hurley, Cheryl Lundstrom, Irene Zahava, and Sherry Redding in the past and present. In that time, we've lost some important writers, but not their voices. These women are with me every day. ∾

Melanie Perish is a writer, editor, teacher and student. Born in Chicago, resident of Matteson, Illinois, Bloomington, Indiana, New York City, and Panguitch, Utah, she is glad to call Nevada home. She regularly travels to the San Francisco Bay Area, Santa Fe, and Texas. Melanie is grateful for her friends, family, recovery, and all who continue to fight for social justice. <u>Passions & Gratitudes</u> (Black Rock Press, 2011), a collection of her poetry, and <u>The Fishing Poems</u> (Chapbook, Meridian Press, 2017) are recent publications. She is a member of Poets & Writers, Inc., continues to do poetry readings, and has done Poets-in-the-Schools. She's grateful for mindfulness, poetry, work, science, engineering, and other people. Melanie lives in the rain shadow of the Sierra Nevada mountains. She believes reading makes you beautiful.

∽

Designed at Creek Crest Publishing by Sunny B.
The text font is Caslon and Myriad Pro as display.

Madrina Editions
Single Wing Press